Fragrance

of GRACE

My Journey to

Freedom and Wholeness

Rita Baroni

"Fragrance of Grace"
Rita Baroni
1ˢᵗ Edition 2008
Copyright: Kingdomsongs Inc.

Book design by
Treasure Image & Publishing
TreasureImagePublishing.com
248.403.8046

Dedication

David, you have been God's most tangible
fragrance of grace to me. You have loved me
well. I am glad that you are my love!

Bethany, you bring joy to all who know you. You carry the
peace of the Lord. I love worshiping the Lord with you!

Ben, you are a gift to Bethany and to our family. Your
passion for God and life are an inspiration to me! I am
glad you are my son-in-law!

Charity, your love of people and life spreads the fragrance of
God everywhere you are! I love and miss you so much!

Celeste, you bring compassion and grace into this
world! You are a well of deep living water! I love
hearing you sing and laugh! I love you!

Jesus, for loving me and putting your fragrance of grace in me.
You have turned death into life and changed my mourning into
dancing. You are my first Love!

Thank You! Thank you!

*"And when we obey Him, every path He guides us on
is fragrant with His loving-kindness and truth"*
Psalm 25:10 TLB

TABLE OF CONTENTS

Fragrance

"Thanks to God, who always leads us in triumph in Christ, and manifests through us the sweet aroma of the knowledge of Him in every place. For we are a fragrance of Christ to God, among those who are being saved and among those who are perishing."
(II Corinthians 2:14, 15)

Jesus is the fragrance of life to me. I don't know how to explain it. I just know when I am breathing His presence in, there is an aroma I can't describe. There are people who represent Christ's fragrance to me too. When I am with them I am refreshed. Flowers and trees bring me close to God with their fragrance. And the aroma of certain foods can take me back to places and times gone by. The smell of certain desserts makes my mouth water before they are finished baking. I have great visits with my friends over a cup of aromatic herbal tea.

When my mom was in the hospital dying of cancer, I would spend hours there every day. I would go home in the late afternoon and take long walks around my neighborhood to clear the smells out of my head. This was in May and the Magnolia trees were in full bloom and the honeysuckle was growing everywhere. God must have known at creation that I would need those fragrances to give me life. I can smell a magnolia or honeysuckle and sense the Presence of God.

This book is about God's fragrance of redemption and restoration throughout my life. There are people who have been the very aroma of Christ to me. I will share some of them with you in these pages. There are places where the Lord has met me that I go back to time and again just to breathe God's breath there.

Several years ago my husband, David, and I were in New York speaking and singing at a conference. I was in a dry place spiritually. I wasn't enjoying life. I was praying hard and seeking God but still stuck. And there I was "ministering." I asked God to bless His Word and the people I was ministering to, because it wasn't their fault I was in a hard place. After one of the services an elderly lady came up to me with a gift. She said that the Lord told her to give these to me. One was an empty perfume vial in the shape of a rose and the other was a small jewelry box with a rose on it. She said that I was an empty vessel used by the Lord, and that the fragrance from the Rose of Sharon-Jesus came out of me. I had been praying II Corinthians 2:14, 15, to be a fragrance of the Lord. God is faithful!

Beginnings

Lately, I've been thinking about Chicago, where I was born. I remember playing in the big concrete backyard and walking home to Maw Maw's from school for lunch. I remember getting sent home from kindergarten for beating up a boy (he started it; I promise).

I remember going to the liquor store for candy and hearing the sirens at night across the street at The Pink Dragon Tavern. I remember putting on my big snow suit and snow boots and not being able to breathe except through the two holes in the front of my hood. I remember the store front Pentecostal church where they let me play the tambourine during song service.

I can't remember how many apartments we lived in during my seven short years there. I know I went to six different schools by the end of 2nd grade. I've been thinking about our move to Kentucky into our three room house. We lived across the yard from Grandma and her chickens. We watched the bats fly around the one light pole and saw the snakes coming down from the mountain, going by the front porch to get to the pond at the foot of the mountain by our house. I was sitting safely in Grandma's lap on the porch swing.

Bathing in the tin tub wasn't so bad as long as I was the first one to get a bath before my sister, brother and mom while the water was the cleanest. I loved being wrapped in the towel and warming myself by the coal stove, then getting into bed with lots of covers. I can still smell the food from the cafeteria at Totz Elementary School. Sometimes it was actually edible.

Summer came, and with it the long trip to Chicago to live there again for awhile. Then we moved to Missouri to live for a few months. That was a very scary time for me as a six year old, and the memories are sad. We moved back to Chicago. I can still feel the fear as we were being sent home from school because of riots in the streets because Martin Luther King, Jr. got shot. Mom and Dad wanted to get us away from the Big City, so we took a long ride to Alabama to live there.

Our first house in Alabama had a cotton field in the front yard and an outhouse in the backyard. It was fun playing outside so much and having a warm Christmas. Picking cotton wasn't so much fun in the summer. It was hot and sticky and I was afraid of the wasps. I did get to stay in the same school for a couple of years, though.

I've been thinking about the little Baptist Church where I went up to the altar to pray. I loved Vacation Bible School and the crafts and cookies and the red Koolaid. I went to lots of churches growing up, and I loved them all. I loved the flannelgraph board, singing

Onward Christian Soldiers and marching into Sunday night children's church at the Presbyterian church across the street from our house in Tuscumbia. I loved riding the church bus that took us to the Missionary Baptist church in Florence (we got candy to eat on the way). The Church of God gave me lots of friends and youth camps and winter retreats.

Lately, I've been thinking about how God has brought me through it all, been with me in it all and has a purpose for it all. Lately, I've been thinking about God's love and faithfulness.

> *"For you have been my hope O, God. You are my confidence from my youth. By You I have been sustained from my birth. You took me from my mother's womb."*
> (Psalm 71:5,6)

So, here is the start of my journey on the road to healing, wholeness, rebellion, forgiveness, fear, faith, hope and freedom. I welcome you to come along with me on the journey of finding God on this road. My prayer for you is that you will smell the fragrance of Christ in the pages of this book. May He breathe redemption and restoration into your life. Remember, you are a fragrant aroma of Christ!

Chicago

Norma Charlene Robinson married Bobby Ray Phillips in September 1959. My mom and dad already had a 14 month old little girl when I was born. Freida Gail was born April 24, 1960. I, Rita Kaye, was born June 20, 1961. Four and a half years after me came the first son, David Alan, born October 14, 1965. Then January 6, 1971 another son was born, Nolan John. Our family was complete. My parents moved a lot, so Freida and Nolan were born in Alabama. David and I were born in Chicago.

Grace and Shame

Grace is abundant and open and lavished on me from Father God to heal and save me. Shame is sneaky and hidden and jumps out of nowhere to scare me and consume me. There have been many times in my life where I was shamed. Some of the shaming was intentional; most of it was not. I hear stories about my infancy that I can't remember but somehow cause me to feel ashamed when I hear them.

The doctor who delivered me was drunk and barely caught me when I was born. As a child, I was skinny and sickly. I was in the hospital when I was about two years old with a very high fever for days. I had boils on my head. Because of the fever my hair fell out.

I attended six different schools by the end of second grade. When I was in third grade, the secretary of the school announced over the PA system for the students who received free lunch cards to go to the school office. I was so ashamed that I couldn't afford to buy my lunch that I did not go to the school office and went hungry that week. We got government food and food stamps when I was young.

When I was a teenager my parents divorced. Even though it wasn't my fault, I was ashamed. I am a product of my growing up years. It has taken lots of grace and love from God to heal me. One of my favorite books on the grace of God to heal shame is *"Shame Off You"* by Alan D. Wright. I laughed. I cried. I prayed. I healed.

"But you will be called the priests of the Lord. You will be spoken of as ministers of our God. You will eat the wealth of nations. Instead of your shame you will have double honor. And instead of humiliation you will shout for joy over their portion. Therefore you will possess a double portion in their land. Everlasting joy will be yours. For I, the Lord, love justice."
(Isaiah 61:6,7,8a)

Living in the City

I have never liked the cold. I shiver at the thought of being cold. So walking to school and church as a little girl in the winter is still a vivid memory. I can remember my snow suit and boots keeping everything but my nose and eyes warm. I have five coats in my closet right now. I also have five neck scarves and three pair of leather gloves. Even though I live in Nashville where we only have one month of really cold weather, I am prepared in case the windy city blows its cold winds my way.

When I was young, the aunts, uncles and cousins spent a lot of time together. The cousins would play in the backyard of the apartment building, or if it was too cold we would play in the living room of Maw Maw's house. The children were four to seven years of age. We would dance to music in the livingroom, mostly Elvis and country music.

One summer day Freida and I were playing outside. I went in to check on my bird. It was in the bottom of the cage. It was cold. In my five year old mind all I could think of was to get the bird warm and he wouldn't be dead. So, I turned on the oven and put the bird in it. Thankfully, my mom found out what I did before we had baked bird that afternoon.

There were gangs in the nearby neighborhoods and sometimes we would be rushed inside to be safe. My cousin was almost attacked by a gang. He ran home in a panic. He hid for hours in the basement. I remember playing in the backyard of our apartment building. We would play hopscotch and baseball (with a plastic bat and ball) and ride our bikes with the neighborhood kids. I loved double-dutch jump rope. We played until dark. There were always lots of kids around.

When I was in school in 2nd grade, we were sent home because of riots in the streets. Martin Luther King, Jr. had been shot. I didn't really know what was going on except that everyone was scared. Mom and dad were at work, so the babysitter picked my sister and me up and walked us across the street to our apartment. We didn't live long at that apartment. Mom and Dad wanted to get us out of the big city. We left aunts and uncles and cousins to move south.

Totz

In Totz, Kentucky as of 2007 the population is 580. Totz is the town I lived in when I was six. We moved there because my parents separated and that is where Grandma lived. She had a three bedroom house with a living room and kitchen and an "outhouse" for a bathroom. That means we had to walk out of the house and go to the backyard to a tiny room that looked like a wooden closet to go to the bathroom. I always hated to go to the bathroom at night because I was afraid of the dark and snakes and wasps. I begged my sister to go with me and hold the flashlight.

There was a three room house across the yard from Grandma that my mom, sister, brother and I moved into. We had a living room, kitchen and bedroom (and an outhouse). There was a coal stove in the living room. At night in the winter we put a sheet up between the living room and kitchen so the bedroom would get more heat. We would play outside from sunrise to sunset.

We lived on the side of the mountain, literally. There was one road that ran from Cumberland to Harlan and it went through Totz. You either lived up the mountain on one side of the road, or you lived down the mountain on the other side of the road. There was a pond at the foot of the mountain by the railroad tracks. The snakes would slither by our three room house to get to the pond. I would sit on the porch swing and when I saw a snake I would run into the house.

Grandma would hoe her potatoes and throw them into a bucket. We would wash them later and we would have them for supper. I can still see her 5 foot 3 inch strong body with a dress down to her ankles and sleeves past her elbows and shoe boots and a hat. She wasn't afraid of the snakes at all. She would see one and kill it with the hoe and finish getting her potatoes.

I loved the seemingly 10 foot tall sunflowers that grew in Grandma's yard. They were bright yellow and beautiful. One time I started chasing one of Grandma's chickens and the rooster started chasing me. I was so scared I literally almost ran over the hill and down the side of the mountain to my death. Grandma caught me just in time.

One of my favorite memories is going to church. We had to walk a couple of miles to get to church. It was a white wood building sitting on the side of the mountain. The front part of the building was on cinder blocks and the back part was on wood stilts. There was a coal stove and hard wooden benches, a very old piano and an outhouse. I seldom went to the bathroom when I went to church.

It was a Pentecostal Church and Brother Shell was the preacher. Sister Ellen would sing "specials" before the preaching. A "special" is a very anointed song to get the Spirit of God moving so we would be ready for the Word of God to be preached. I loved it when she would sing:

"He made the rocks; He made the trees
Tell me who but God could do such things as these
He made the clouds; He made the rain
He is great and He is worthy of all praise!"

Sister Ellen was a powerful woman who would play her guitar until a string broke and would dance across the stage under the power of God until her long hair would fly all over the place and her face would turn red. Oh, how I wanted to be able to sing like her! It has been 40 years since I heard her and I can still sing the words of that song.

Totz Elementary is where I attended part of first grade. We rode the school bus around the curvy road and over the bumps, and if I had to sit in the back of the bus I would get motion sickness. The cafeteria smelled like dirty mop water most of the time. Some days it smelled like bleach. I didn't like eating in the cafeteria because of those smells. My children accuse me of having a way-too-sensitive nose.

The lady up the mountain made school clothes for me and my sister. I was so excited to help pick out the material for my new clothes! My favorite pair of pants were blue with white stars around the hem.

I was a very active child and mischievous. One time during recess we were playing hide and seek. I figured the perfect place to hide, so I got in my locker and shut the door. No one could find me and I was glad, until I realized NO ONE could find me. I started banging on the locker door and screaming to be let out. Finally, a teacher came and told me to calm down and she would let me out. Well, it is very hard to calm down when you are six years old trapped in a dark small locker. I got in a lot of trouble when I got home.

Freida and I would play in the woods beside our house and put our feet in the tiny little stream that went down the side of the mountain. Hide and seek was lots of fun. In the winter, our family chopped down our Christmas tree in the back of the woods. The winter was cold and snowy. The woods were absolutely majestic with the snow on the trees.

I loved going into "town" on Saturdays. We would get fresh okra and corn. There weren't any big supermarkets, just home owned grocery stores where everyone knew everyone's name. From what I can remember, everyone knew everyone's business too. We would go to the Feed Store to get chicken feed and seeds to plant in the garden.

The store smelled like a barn and for some reason I liked that smell. When there was enough money we would go to the Dairy King and get a nickel ice cream! Grandma would charge her purchases to "store credit" and sign her name that she would pay off the bill her next pay check. Grandma didn't work in a public job, so I always wondered where her paycheck came from.

I would walk up the dirt road to put the mail in the mailbox and leave just enough change for the stamps for the mailman to put on the mail.

When the sun went down in Totz it was dark, I mean really dark. There was one light pole up the hill not too far from the front of the house. The bats would fly around it at night. I would sit on the front porch swing and listen to the bats fly and the crickets sing. I enjoyed the noises of the night. I loved starry nights and full moons.

We moved back to Chicago after our months in Totz. I went back to visit Grandma for the summer, when I was 13. She wanted me to live with her for awhile. She fried okra, potatoes and chicken. We went to church together. By this time Brother Shell had retired and we went to another Pentecostal Church. It was too far to walk, so someone would pick us up. This church aired their Sunday morning church services on the radio. I was asked to sing a special before the preacher preached his sermon. Since I would never be as good as Sister Ellen, I chose a different song to sing on the radio. I can't remember the name of the song, but it had the words "He gives me faith to make it."

A lot of people there were very afraid of going to hell. They tried to please God by the clothes they wore, by how long the women's hair was, or how short the men's hair was, or how many kids you had. So, at 13 I decided that I would not cut my hair or wear pants because God wanted women to look like women not men. I quit wearing jewelry because I didn't want to have a proud spirit. I wouldn't wear makeup because I should be content with how I look. I don't want to be judgmental; I love my heritage!

Those precious people loved God with all their hearts and very much wanted to please Him. That is what they were taught, and they were being obedient. When I moved back home after that summer, I realized that I could wear pants and make up (yay!) and still have God's approval.

My days spent in Totz are mostly good memories for me. I lived a simpler life. Even though the outhouse wasn't my favorite part of living there, it makes for good stories and lots of laughter.

Missouri

We moved again when I was about six or seven. My parents had separated once more, and this time we ended up in Missouri living with a friend of my mom's. She didn't like children very much, and mom had three children. There was always a lot of tension in the house. Freida and I walked to and from school every day. We had to walk by a cemetery to get to school. In the daylight it wasn't so bad, but when it was not fully light in the morning it was scary.

Mom was under a lot of pressure to provide for us financially and to keep three children behaving perfectly for the lady we were living with. One evening at dinner my sister and I were playing with our food and the mean old lady said, "I can't believe you let your children be so disrespectful." Well, that was all it took to send my mom into panic. This was the only place she could think of to live safely. To prove she was in control and that her children would not be out of control, my mom disciplined us. The memory of being stripped and beaten still makes my heart quiver sometimes.

I know now as an adult that it was fear that drove her to do that. However, as a little girl I realized I did not have a safe place to live or a safe person to live with. I cried many tears over those months in Missouri.

The only answer I have come up with so far is that I lived through it. I have healed and there are no scars on my body left. The scars from my heart are healed too. God's grace is sufficient to heal and to take the power of the pain of the memory away. Today, I am grateful to be alive and to have wholeness in my spirit and soul.

"O God, You have taught me from my youth, and I still declare Your wondrous deeds. Even when I am old and gray, O God do not forsake me. I will declare your strength to this generation and Your power to all who are to come."
(Psalm 71:17,18)

Boondocks

I realize that some of you reading this book are highly educated and live in the city, so you might not know what boondocks means. Here is the definition from Webster's College dictionary:

> **boondocks:** noun, 1. an uninhabited area such as a backwoods or marsh 2. a remote rural area (a locative derivation as "the sticks").

When my family moved from the big city of Chicago, the boondocks is precisely where we landed. We moved into a house in Rogersville, AL. We had a beautiful view of the sky from our bedroom ceiling. Actually, the wall and ceiling didn't meet in the corner. We could see part of the sky. We had a bathroom that was located in the backyard, an outhouse. It wasn't furnished with running water. It did have an ample supply of spider webs though. I have confirmed the condition of our first Alabama house with my dad's cousin. It was every bit as backwoods and scary as my mind remembers.

Then we moved to Tuscumbia. This town is where Helen Keller was born. It had a town square and a grocery store. Our house was old but it had an inside bathroom with running water! It was an oblong house. You had to walk through the livingroom and two bedrooms to get to the kitchen. My sister and I shared a bedroom. My mom, dad and two brothers shared another bedroom. There wasn't much privacy, but I was only eight years old and didn't need much privacy.

Being born in Chicago and having gone to elementary school with many children of different ethnicities, I was used to different accents. None of the accents that I was used to hearing sounded like southern accents. I equated being poor and dumb with being Southern. I apologize to all the wealthy and very intelligent people who are from the South. I enjoy southern accents and southern charm now. My girls were born and raised in Tennessee. They are intelligent and on their way to becoming wealthy.

I guess the reason I thought of people living in the south as being poor is because we became poor in Alabama. We had to have food stamps and government food given to us monthly. We got free lunches at school. People donated clothes to us at Christmas. My mom worked at a clothing factory. My dad drove a truck for a cookie distributor. My favorite Christmas present when I was young was my pink quilted house coat (robe) from my mom.

We lived in the house in Tuscumbia for three years. I have good memories of playing in the front yard with my friends and riding my bicycle on the sidewalk around the block. We didn't get to see our Chicago relatives much, though.

Then we moved to Sheffield, AL. My parents bought a three bedroom brick home. I thought we had a mansion. My sister and I shared a bedroom. My brothers shared a bedroom. My mom and dad had their own bedroom.

By this time we no longer needed free lunches or government food. I started babysitting and was able to buy clothes for myself. While living in Sheffield my parents divorced. They always fought and didn't get along. We had moved away from Chicago to start a new life. We really just brought the old one with us. The fighting and screaming just got worse. I was actually glad when they divorced. I was hoping for some peace and quiet. I felt very responsible for my younger brothers because my mother worked from 4 p.m. until midnight.

For a long time after I married, I didn't want to go back to Alabama. Mom had moved to Missouri. Dad and I didn't keep in touch at that time. The painful memories overshadowed the good memories. I know that there were many good things that happened. Over the years I have become grateful for my childhood and my experiences. I see that I am stronger and more compassionate. I have let God show me that my life has a purpose. There were many people that carried the fragrance of the grace of God to me in those moments of my life. I would not be alive today without them.

A couple of years ago David and I were invited to a church in Florence, Alabama to do a worship conference. I was asked to speak and teach. I was excited and nervous. You see Florence is the city right next to Sheffield. The church was ten minutes from the house where I grew up. I was praying about what I was supposed to teach. I didn't feel anything specific, so I closed my notebook and turned on some music. I was washing dishes when a song got my attention. I knew then what I was supposed to share. Because of not ever having enough as a child, I felt like I was never enough as a teenager or adult. I never felt pretty enough or smart enough or rich enough or popular enough. I couldn't see value in myself. I had fairly good grades in high school. I had friends. I was in all the clubs at school. I was an officer in almost all of those clubs. I was the president of choir my senior year. I was on homecoming court. But it didn't seem like it was enough. The Lord started healing me, and I started receiving value as His daughter. Finally, a Father who loved me and provided for me and thought I was wonderful! He even gave me my personality! Today, I realize that I *am* enough.

Oh yeah, the song that was my sermon title: Boondocks by the group Little Big Town. It is a country song. (I do live in Nashville. It is a requirement for me to listen to country music sometimes). I listened to that song over and over. It touched a place deep in my soul. I had carried such guilt and shame. I was being freed from it, and this song at this time in my life was part of the fragrance of God's healing to me. After I spoke at the conference that afternoon a lot of people went to the store and bought that CD. I believe that God used these words to help others heal too. Whatever your "boondocks" looks like, God can meet you in that isolated backwoods place. He will even meet you in the outhouse if that is where you are!

"Boondocks"

"I feel no shame I'm proud of where I came from
I was born and raised in the boondocks
One thing I know, no matter where I go
I keep my heart and soul in the boondocks

I can feel that muddy water running through my veins
I can hear that lullaby of the midnight train
And it sings to me and it sounds familiar
I can taste that honeysuckle and it's still so sweet
When it grows wild
On the banks down at old camp creek
It calls to me like a warm wind blowing

It's where I learned about living
It's where I learned about love

It's where I learned about working hard and having a little
is just enough
It's where I learned about Jesus
And knowing where I stand
You can take it or leave it
This is me- this is who I am

Give me a tin roof, a front porch and a gravel road
And that's home to me; feels like home to me
I feel no shame. I'm proud of where I came from
I was born and raised in the boondocks
One thing I know, now matter where I go
I keep my heart and soul in the boondocks."

Words and Music:Wayne Kirkpatrick, Kimberly Roads, Phillip Sweet,
Karen Fairchild, Jimi Westbrook
2004 Warner Tamerlane Publishing / Sell the Cow Music/Tower One
Music/WB Music Corp ./ Tower Two/ ASCAP

Meeting David

I started working at Kentucky Fried Chicken in Sheffield, AL when I was fifteen. After being there one year I transferred to Muscle Shoals KFC. I loved my job, my employer and my co-workers. For a bunch of teenagers, we were actually pretty responsible. We cooked; we waited on customers; we cleaned; and we ate lots of chicken. My favorite things to eat were the little bucket desserts! I worked there for three years while I was in high school and through one year of college.

Right after I graduated from high school a good-looking guy came in to eat. He was friendly. His name was David. We started talking and I found out that he was a musician. He was a piano player! This got my attention because I was the Youth Choir Director at our church. The pianist was inconsistent in coming to practice, so I was praying for another person to help. I invited him to my church. I had to inform him about our church. I am from a Pentecostal background. We prayed out loud. We sang out loud. We fellowshipped out loud. The preacher preached out loud. Pretty much every thing we did was loud! I loved my church and most everything about it. However, I didn't want David to be scared.

People were friendly and welcoming to him. He enjoyed the music. He listened to the preaching. He didn't leave when we all prayed out loud at the same time! At the end of the service, after hearing a 14 year old testify, David went to the altar to pray and to ask Jesus to come into his heart and to forgive his sins. The testimony of the 14 year old was simple and clear, "I just want to thank Jesus for dying on the cross for me, for getting those nails in his hands so that I could be saved." The boy who gave that testimony is my brother Dave.

David had lots of questions about the Bible, about salvation and about a lot of spiritual things. I had to do a lot of Bible study to answer those questions. We grew very close as friends. We were dating also. After David asked the Lord into his heart, he didn't want to be in the studio scene anymore. He quit the band and didn't have a job. He moved back to Natchez, MS, where he was born and raised and where his parents still lived. We quit dating but remained friends.

He moved to Nashville to pursue Contemporary Christian music. He came back to Alabama to play for our Youth Choir in an outdoor concert. We started talking about dating again and before we knew it we were planning the date for our wedding.

We didn't have any counseling. We didn't have any money. We didn't have any mentors. We were going to live on love. After the wedding I moved to Nashville with my new husband. He had an apartment in a scary part of town. We were happy; we were broke, and we were in love. We had one car and no phone. We also had no credit cards, no car payment and no debt. We just had living expenses. We had a bed, a couch, a kitchen table and a piano. And remember we had love. David worked the midnight shift. I worked the day shift. I slept while he worked. He slept while I worked. We had dinner together at night. Our apartment was robbed while we were out of town. They took our little television and David's guitar. That is all that we owned that had any resale value. One night while David was at work a man wishing to purchase drugs banged on our front door and scared me half to death. But it was the rat that greeted me in the kitchen one morning that made me decide it was time to move to another apartment. Our first Christmas tree was given to us and it had one ornament on it.

That was 28 years ago. We have a lot more now. We have three wonderful children, one wonderful son-in-law, a home, lots of furniture, lots of bills, some debt, a home phone, a cell phone and a dog. We have history. Like most people, our story contains sadness and tragedy, loss and regret. It also contains great joys and victories, hope and laughter. The one thing that we still have is love. We still have each other, and I am so glad! One of my favorite scriptures that represents my marriage and my children is this:

"Everyone who hears these words of Mine and acts on them, may be compared to a wise man who built his house on the Rock. The rain fell and the floods came, and the winds blew and slammed against that house; yet it did not fall, for it had been founded on the rock."
Matthew 7:24,25.

We have taught at Marriage Conferences and Retreats. We speak from a place of experience, healing and truth. We know what it is like to need help and not know where to find it. We are grateful to the people who have walked with us along our journey. They have prayed and cried and laughed with us (and laughed at us). They let us know that we would make it. They also gave us tools to build our house. When David and I got married it was like we were put in a field full of rocks and dirt and told to build a house. We didn't know how to build a house. After awhile we just picked up the rocks and started throwing them at each other. David and I did have a rocky start, but we truly did have our foundation built on the Rock, Jesus. I am grateful to our Rock of Salvation for saving us in the midst of all the storms of life. I am grateful and blessed.

Velma and Earl

Velma and Earl brought joy to my life. They were an elderly couple. They were married for many years. We went to the same church in Nashville. When the offering plate would be passed, Earl would hand the usher a quarter and ask for change back. One time he started kissing Velma's ear during the service. Well, she would have none of that in church, so she yelled out loud, "Earl, stop that! We are in church!"

Later on, Earl got sick and started losing weight. He also had to use crutches to walk because his balance was off. One Sunday he had to go to the bathroom during the church service. He got up and started walking to the back of the church. He lost his balance and his pants fell down around his ankles. We heard the commotion going on and looked around just in time to see one of the deacons grab Earl's pants and usher him through the swinging doors to the bathroom. By this time Earl was disoriented and forgot to close the bathroom door. A few moments later we heard him--well, I won't go into any more detail. The congregation was trying to ignore the whole situation, but the pastor burst into laughter. After we all had a good laugh, the sermon was cut short and we went home early.

David and I lived across the street from Velma and Earl for a few months. In the middle of the night we heard someone banging on our bedroom window. It scared us. Velma was screaming, "Earl fell! Come help!" David ran across the street. Earl was lying on the floor of the bathroom propped up on his elbow. When David walked in Earl greeted him with a big smile and welcomed him in. He thought David was there for a neighborly 3 a.m. visit!

Velma had a wringer washer that broke, so I took her to the local appliance store to buy another one. She did not go to the big chain store-super center stores. She supported the local merchants. The local store tried to convince her that the newer automatic washer was much more convenient. She wanted what she had always used (since she quit using a wash tub and scrub board). A week later her brand new wringer washer was delivered. She hung her clothes on the clothes line in the back yard. She ironed all of her bed linens and her undergarments. I would visit Velma and Earl often. Their house always smelled like liniment and vapor rub and fried chicken. We would have them over for holiday meals. She brought fried pies. She always wore a house dress and had her 50 strands of hair pulled back in a pony tail. I miss her and what she represented: determination, loyalty, faith, laughter and innocence. She always enjoyed a good joke and she loved to laugh!

Sister Ward and Sister Gracie were sisters who went to our church. They did not miss a church service, ladies get-together, church picnic, yard sale or any function the church hosted. They lived 45 minutes from the church. We would take turns picking them up for services. Gracie was the baby of the family. She would always let us know that she was younger in front of her older sister. Gracie was 84 and Sister Ward was 86. They were fiesty and fun and full of life.

We had a lot of elderly people at our little church. They helped remind all of us "twenty-somethings" that life is precious and that we too would not always be young. I wish my girls who are in their 20's could be around the elderly more. There was something sacred about taking them to the grocery store and just sitting in their homes and listening to their stories.

Abundant Grace

Bethany Rozan

Bethany, you're precious to your daddy and me
You're so full of life and full of love
Bethany, you're the beautiful melody
In a song that has been given from above
Bethany so sweet, you make our lives complete
And we thank our God above
For sending you our precious love
We love you, Bethany

Bethany, you look like daddy, you look like me
You're our special gift from God, you see.
Bethany, welcome to the family
Jesus smiles upon us, Bethany

Bethany was born January 7, 1984 at 8:05 p.m. Her name means God's dwelling-Rose. She weighed 6 lbs. 12 oz. and was 21 ½ inches long. She was eager to start her life outside of confinement in the womb; she was born after only two hours of labor. She came kicking and screaming into this world. She wanted to let us know that she had arrived. We were so glad that she was here! Beautiful blue eyes, fuzzy dark hair, long eyelashes. She was a beauty. She still is. As a baby she loved to be cuddled and fed. Did I mention that she liked to be fed? By six months she weighed 21 pounds. She was intelligent too. She loved for me to read to her. She enjoyed playing with her paper dolls and baby dolls.

When Bethany was about a year and a half old David and I decided we wanted another baby. When I was five months pregnant, I miscarried. It was very sad. After that, David felt like we didn't need any more children. I didn't agree, so I surprised him a few months later and told him we were going to have a baby. (Okay, so I don't recommend doing this, but it worked out fine). He was excited, and we started planning for another baby! I had an ultrasound at six weeks and the baby was healthy. I had another ultrasound at five months and found out that it was a girl! We were glad that Bethany would have a baby sister.

My tummy grew quite large and people would comment on it. At the grocery store someone asked me how many I had in there. I would bump into things and Bethany would try to push my stomach out of the way. I was so big I could use my tummy as a table and put my plate on it. I went into labor five and 1/2 weeks early. I was at church and noticed that I was having contractions. A group of us went out to eat after church. They helped me time my contractions. I ate a huge meal before I went to the hospital because I didn't want to be hungry during labor. We got to the hospital at 9:00 p.m. They hooked me up to a monitor to time the contractions. I forgot how intense natural childbirth was with Bethany, so I did natural again. I guess I had memory loss. After being in labor for twelve hours the doctor broke my water. Ten minutes later Charity Lynne (her name means flowing brook of love) was born! She weighed 5 pounds 2 ounces and was 19 inches long. She was having difficulty breathing, so they took her to another part of the room and were working with her. David was taking pictures.

I was still in pain and told my doctor that my back was still hurting. She said to push and get the afterbirth out. I pushed and another bag of water broke. My doctor said, "Lord, I don't believe this. There is another baby in there!" David said, "You're kidding!" She wasn't kidding. My room filled with more nurses and medical equipment. I promptly told the doctor, "Give me drugs." She told me it was too late, so I told her, "You get the baby out." She told me I had to push. The sweet nurse holding my hand told me that I could do this. Somehow, I believed her. Eight minutes later Celeste Gabrielle (her name means heavenly messenger) was born. She weighed 4 pounds 9 ounces and was 17 1/2 inches long. I did it! I had twins naturally.

Charity and Celeste

Charity Lynne, where do we begin
To tell you of our love
Celeste Gabrielle, our little angel
Sent to us from God above
We'll kiss away your tears, protect you from your fears
And love you through the years
We'll watch you while you play, teach you how to pray
And guide you on your way

Charity Lynne, where do we begin
To tell you of our love
Celeste Gabrielle, our little angel
Sent to us from God above
And now we give you to the One who gave us you
Abundantly we're blessed
With Bethany, Charity and Celeste

We went home three days later and began our journey of many sleepless nights with feedings every two hours. Bethany needed to be nurtured and fed. She was only three years and one month old when her baby sisters were born. She thought that we had brought her live baby dolls to play with. She would hold them, change their diapers (as long as they weren't the stinky kind), sing to them and help put their clothes on them.

Charity was born moving and hasn't stopped. She crawled. She climbed out of her baby bed. She went up and down the stairs continually. She pushed Celeste around in the walker. She was active.

Testing

Celeste's motor skills didn't develop as quickly. Everyone kept telling us not to compare twins. At their one year doctor's visit, the pediatrician said that Celeste's motor skills were not developed enough and that she needed to see a neurologist. She wasn't sitting up on her own, crawling or standing. After tests and tears, she was diagnosed with Cerebral Palsy. The oxygen or blood flow had been cut off to the back of her brain while she was in the womb. She had no spine control. She couldn't hold her head up very well. She had very little gross motor skills. We were told that she probably would never walk or run and that she would be in a wheelchair the rest of her life. She would need occupational therapy and physical therapy. Then the neurologist ended with "One good thing is that Celeste appears to be very smart."

One day after having Celeste in therapy, I was tired and sad. I called a friend to have her pray for me. I told her what the doctor had said. She then responded with "What good is it if she is smart, if she is going to be in a wheelchair the rest of her life?" I didn't know how to respond, so I just told her thanks for her prayers. I was angry and went upstairs to pray. I told the Lord, "Your Word says that your grace is sufficient, and right now I need an abundance of your grace! I don't care if Celeste ever walks on this earth as long as I know she will run in Heaven. Lord, she is yours!" I felt the very tangible presence of the Lord.

By this time, Celeste had crawled into the room where I was praying. The only way she could crawl was to lie flat on her tummy and pull with her arms, like an army crawl. I picked her up and cried and gave her back to the Lord. She played with my tears. I felt abundant grace come over me. I knew that no matter what happened somehow God would take care of both of us.

That night Celeste stood up and held onto the piano bench. The next day she crawled up the stairs in our home. The day after that she started crawling on her hands and knees. I thought to myself that the Lord must be healing her. I took her to physical therapy and occupational therapy that Friday. I didn't go into the nurse's room with her for therapy because it hurt my heart to see my baby cry because the therapy was painful.

After several minutes the nurse came out and said "You brought me the wrong twin!" I told her that she indeed was Celeste. She said, "But there is not one tight muscle in this baby's body." I finally was able to tell her that I thought the Lord was healing her. She said, "If this is Celeste then the Lord must be healing her!"

Celeste was scheduled for a CAT scan of her brain the following Monday. David and I took her to the neurologist's office. It was hard watching her be put to sleep. She fought going to sleep. I cried. I was numb. David and I waited. After she came out of the scan, we took her home. Then we waited some more. The next day the doctor called and said, "Mrs. Baroni, I don't know what to tell you. We can't find anything wrong with Celeste. We can't find anything wrong with her brain or her motor skills. I am going to release her, unless you want to keep bringing her in." I told her thanks and that we would not be bringing her back in. It was real. Celeste was healed!

God had breathed His breath of life into her brain. He took what was dead and made it alive. She was standing. She was walking. She was healed! I prayed for God's grace that day. In His grace He chose to heal her, because He loves her and delights in her. He gets all the glory.

"Surely our griefs He Himself bore and our sorrows He carried. Yet we esteemed Him stricken, smitten of God and afflicted. But He was pierced through for our transgressions. He was crushed for our iniquities. The chastening for our well being fell upon Him. And by His scourging we are healed! (Isaiah 53:4,5)

Life on the Refrigerator

This morning I was walking around my kitchen praying out loud and thanking God for His faithfulness. I looked at the fridge and started praying for all the people in the photographs that covered the door. I realized again what a rich life I have because of family and friends. There is a collage of my family: Bethany and Charity together at Thanksgiving; Celeste and Charity together at Christmas; David, Me, Ben, Bethany, Charity and Celeste together on Christmas Day. I thought back on Christmas Day 2007 and remembered how grateful I was to have the six of us together having Christmas lunch as a family. We opened our gifts and each shared how God had been faithful to us that year and what we were most thankful for. As my children get older and follow God's call on their lives, I realize that the call may have us apart on holidays; so this Christmas was especially meaningful. Celeste was living in Athens, Greece teaching kindergarten at a school for mostly refugee children. She was home for three weeks during Christmas. Charity was in Los Angeles rehearsing for a television show she would be performing on; she was home for only four days for the Christmas holiday. Ben and Bethany were living in a city nearby and were able to spend this Christmas with us, however, the year before they were in England with Ben's family. So, this day is so close to my heart. On the refrigerator are photos of the girls when they were four and seven jumping into a pool on Maui, Hawaii. There is a photo of us as a family with friends in Alaska; we were bundled up in warm coats playing in the snow. Other photos stirred laughter and tears and gladness for the rich life I have lived with family and friends. Every photo has a story behind it. I relive those moments in life every time I stop to look at the faces of everyone on the fridge.

Here are the names and stories of my life on the refrigerator:

Viktor and his family from Latvia: beloved friends that David first met at a conference in St. Petersburg, Russia.

Ols family: lifetime friends- I met Melinda when our oldest children were in 1st grade in 1990.

Peacock family: dear friends, we met in Kuwait, they serve God there, I love them with my heart.

Dave and Janis Nicholson: wonderful parents of our dear Son-in-Law, gifts from God to our family.

Gail, Brian, Trudy, Leto and Stavros: friends from Greece, two of our daughters have served with them in ministry.

Lots of young friends at a going away party for Celeste before she went to Greece.

Beloved family members who remind me of God's sovereignty.

Emily: my beloved niece.

Rozan, Diane, Freida, Bethany and me in Los Angeles to be at the show Charity was on.

Pam and Teresa: Worship Institute fun friends that I share life with.

Hector: Ben and Bethany's Compassion International child.

Jessica: friend of my daughters, missionary to Scotland, 19 years old.

Dudley: the cocker spaniel pet, king of the house.

The Dance War teams: Charity and all her friends from the show.

Thanks for reading the story of my life on the fridge. When I feel alone or left out, all I have to do is look at the faces on my refrigerator and remember that I am loved. Who is on your refrigerator? Who is a part of your heart and life? Where have you been? Who went with you?

Who made you laugh? What made you cry? Your life story is worth telling. It is good even when it is hard. Write me and tell me your story. I would love to hear it!

"And when we obey Him, every path He guides us on is fragrant with His loving-kindness and truth."
(Psalm 25:10 TLB)

Daily Bread

Here I sit on Saturday evening at 6:00 p.m. making myself write this chapter. I have seen the miraculous provision of the Lord throughout my life, and I don't want to be in need again. Somehow I wanted to write this part of the book after I had become debt free and wealthy. After all, I am a minister of the Gospel. I am not supposed to be in need. I believe that God supplies all of my needs, right? People have given love offerings to me, David and our ministry. Someone gave us a mini-van three years ago that we still have. I have spent much of my life believing that God would provide for me but being afraid He wouldn't.

As I was having my devotion last week, I read Matthew 6:8-13. The part about "give us this day, our daily bread," jumped out at me. I felt like the Lord was asking me a few questions. "Do you have a place to live today? Do you have food to eat today? Do you have clothes today? Are you loved today? Are you forgiven today?" The answer to all those questions is yes! It is July 2008 and the news and media tell me that everyone is foreclosing on their homes and that no one will have a job or home. That is not true. Our economy is slow right now. I have to remind myself that I am in God's economy. He provided for us to have a home. He provides for us daily. Sometimes, that provision just doesn't look the way I think it is supposed to.

Several years ago, David and I started overusing credit cards thinking that we would make more money soon. We traveled all over the United States, Europe and other countries ministering. Our children were in private schools and played lots of sports. We kept getting deeper in debt. Finally, we woke up and asked for help. We had to stop using credit cards immediately. We took one last trip to Florida for our girls' spring break and used credit cards to pay for it. (A little rebellion). We had to ask for financial aid from the school. We could only afford for the girls to be in one sport. They paid for any other activity they chose to do. We were counseled to not pay for any more missions trips. We were sad to not be able to go to the countries we loved so dearly. We had developed many friendships with those beloved brothers and sisters. We looked for part time work when we weren't ministering.

Shame grew fast and fierce. It wasn't God's fault that we couldn't pay our debt. We created that debt. I didn't want it to look like God wasn't providing for us. I just didn't like the amount that He was providing. At one point, a friend of mine met me at the gas station and filled up my van. Then she had me go to her home and get a bag of groceries. I was grateful and embarrassed. And I was learning a valuable lesson on reaping what you sow. I was also learning humility.

I wasn't being punished. I was being disciplined. The thought of "I want what I want when I want it" was quickly changing. We never went hungry. We never went homeless. We felt like we had failed our girls. Our pastor told us that we had just taught them the best lesson on not getting into debt. We had to humble ourselves and be honest with the Principal of the school. We told him that our girls would not be able to go there the next year, instead we worked out a financial aid plan. I taught at the school. David coached the girls' basketball team. We told our missionary friends that we would not be able to come for awhile. They raised the funds and had us come anyway. We traveled together overseas more that year than any previous years!

We have repented many times for our foolish spending. God has already forgiven us. We are so close to being out of debt! Many thousands of dollars of bills have been paid. We even know some of the credit card collections personnel by name. Tim from Chase even called to wish us a Merry Christmas last year. We probably paid for his family's Christmas presents!

I am so happy for our friends who have abundant wealth! They are blessers and encouragers. They give much of their income to missionaries and ministries and humanitarian projects. I believe that one day we will have more to give. For now we tithe and support a few ministries. I am determined to be faithful in the small things. In the past, God has put money in our account and no one knew where it came from. But I am tired of seeing provision as being only financial. I have an abundant life!

Today, daily bread for me is a husband and children who love me, friends who care, a church family where I belong, a computer to write my book on, a cell phone to call my daughter in Los Angeles, food for supper, a home with an indoor bathroom- two of them actually, a CD player to play my music and legs to dance.

"This is your Father you are dealing with, and He knows better than you what you need. With a God like this loving you, you can pray very simply. Like this: Our Father in heaven reveal who you are. Set the world right; do what's best- as above, so below. Keep us alive with three square meals. Keep us safe from ourselves and the devil. You're in charge! You can do anything you want! You're ablaze in beauty! Yes! Yes! Yes!"
(Matthew 6:9-13 in The Message)

They Came Back

I was watching a TV program today and two widows from 9/11 were sharing their experiences. They said, "Our husbands got on the planes to fly home and they didn't come back." I thought of all the trips whether by plane, train, car, van or bus that my family and I have made. We all came back home. As I write this, Charity is in Los Angeles at a dance exhibition. Celeste is at a class at college and David is in downtown Nashville at a meeting. It doesn't really occur to me that one of them might not come back home.

David has flown to Singapore, Indonesia, Russia, most of Europe, Australia, Nigeria, Kuwait, Latvia and Romania. I have been to lots of those places with him. He has ridden in cars, trains, buses and even was hit (okay, bumped) by a car in Nigeria, but he has always come back. When Bethany was 17, after she graduated from high school, she flew to Texas to join YWAM (Youth With A Mission) one week after 9/11. Everyone kept telling me how safe it was for her to fly because of the heightened security. My heart didn't feel like she was safe.

Charity and Celeste flew to England for their Senior trip and got home two days before all the subway bombs in London were set off. They had been in the very subway that was bombed. I was a little shaken then too, but still they came back home. I have flown to many countries and begged God to let me get home safely to my husband and children. Every time the prayers were answered. David and I swam with stingrays and he was stung by one that completely pierced his toe a few years ago. Steve Erwin, a man from Australia was stung by one in the heart. He didn't make it back home. I don't think I will ever swim with stingrays again!

There are a few people in my life who haven't come back home. One of the hardest is Allison. The pain was almost unbearable when my seven day-old niece, Allison, didn't get to leave the hospital to come home to her mom and dad. She got to go to Heaven instead. I am grateful for Heaven and eternal life, yet it didn't seem fair. She was beautiful and graceful and could have been a ballerina or basketball player or Valedictorian of her High School Class and a wonderful big sister. Now she is perfect and beautiful and healthy and happy. She will know her mom and dad when they get to Heaven. She will also know her brother Maximus and her little sisters, Isabella and Penelope.

Life is hard when they don't come home. God has promised that we have hope after loss and life after death. He also promises that He will be close to us when we are devastated.

"The righteous cry and the Lord hears and delivers them out of all their troubles. The Lord is near to the broken-hearted and saves those who are crushed in spirit."
(Psalm 34:18, 19)

Butterflies and Bumblebees

I cry when I read about purpose and passion and making a difference. Am I fulfilling my purpose and passion? Am I making a difference? For years I was Bethany, Charity and Celeste's Mom, the Room Mom, the Grade Mom, the Gymnastics Mom and the Basketball Mom. When my parents divorced, my mom informed me that I would have to be my two younger brothers' mom. I was 15 when I got that job. After I got married my husband called me "Eve: The Mother of all Living." I thought this was a compliment and took my job very seriously. I mothered anyone who would let me. I mothered my own children. I took nurturing to heart, and cooked and cleaned and watched my friends' children, the children from children's church and the neighbors' children. I was tired. This wasn't my destiny, but I thought it was my duty.

When I was a little girl, I loved to catch butterflies and listen to birds sing and chase frogs. I enjoyed playing outside and being in nature. I would ride my bicycle around the block and lose track of time just being outside.

I liked sitting in the rain and catching the rain drops on my tongue. I loved to dance until I was exhausted. Those childhood days went by so quickly.

I still love children and receive so much joy watching them play and listening to them talk and sing. My nephew and nieces make my heart glad. They are ages six, four, and three. They bring so much joy to my soul. Sometimes, watching them with their innocence helps me remember to be inquisitive and trusting and wide eyed. I like to ask them questions just to see them process their thoughts and come up with the best answers.

I was molested as a little girl and lost my innocence then. I didn't feel safe after that. I lost something that I didn't have words for as a child. It took years to find words for it as an adult. There has been redemption and healing.

I was snaggle-toothed from falling off a rocking horse at age three. I was sent to the principal's office in kindergarten for beating up a little boy. I aggravated every babysitter until they wouldn't baby-sit for me anymore. I also prayed every day and sang "Jesus loves me this I know for the Bible tells me so." I loved to laugh and play jokes on people. I also got my share of paddlings from teachers for speaking my mind (or as I was told, for smarting off to the teachers). I have found that I was a child full of energy and life and mischievousness. I am still discovering the goodness in myself. My words and songs are being heard by my Heavenly Father. I am seen as lovely by my husband and children and by my Creator. I am now the grownup me. I have learned to be content with how I look and the fact that I talk a lot and that I am still opinionated.

I still love nature and playing outside and walking in the rain. I still love to dance and sing. Life is good.

After Charity and Celeste graduated from High School in 2005, I found myself out of the fulltime Mom job. Celeste went away to college and Charity went away to Athens, Greece. Bethany went away with her husband, Ben. David was still going away on weekends to minister. And part of me went away too.

I was relieved not to have the responsibility of working at the school. I missed not going to all the basketball and lacrosse games and dance competitions. Yet, I was ready for a new season in my life. But what would my job description be? I had laid down the "Mother of All Living" title a few years before and had narrowed my Motherhood to pretty much my own children and the young adults that God put in my life to love and mentor.

This is where Butterflies and Bumblebees come into my life. Caterpillars go through a cocoon to leave their old selves behind to get their wings to fly and even get a new name: *Butterflies.*

Bumblebees aerodynamically should not be able to fly. Their wings are too little and their bodies too big and heavy. Yet, their Creator created them to fly- so they do! I have crawled into the cocoon, gotten alone and quiet and had some time with my Creator. Part of me died in that cocoon and miraculously, more of me came to life in the process. I didn't believe I could fly but God who created me and formed me said, "Yes, you can fly; I promise! I made you to fly." So, I believed Him and now I can fly. I have emerged with wings and have gotten a new name!

"You will be called by a new name which the mouth of the Lord will designate. You will also be a crown of beauty in the hand of the Lord and a royal diadem in the hand of your God. You will no longer be called 'Forsaken'. You will be called, 'My delight is in her...' For the Lord delights in you!"
(Isaiah 62:2)

Dad and Mom

Dad was a redeemed and reconciled child of God. He had a lot to be redeemed from. He grew up in a family with five children and lots of cousins and relatives around. There was a lot of love. There was alcoholism too. It got passed down to my dad. When dad wasn't drinking he was fun and jovial and had lots of friends. When he was drinking he was a different person. He would be violent and unpredictable. Usually he would pass out and sleep for a long time. These are the childhood memories that I have of my dad. My adult memories are better. Dad is finally at true peace and reconciled to His Father. The following is the eulogy I gave at my Dad's funeral service. It was actually a celebration of his life! Dad is having one big party in heaven!

Bobby Ray Phillips:
8/3/1939---1/15/2006

Dad, Paw Paw, Bobby, Bobby Ray, Brother, Friend, Buddy. He was called by many names. The Lord called him Child of God.

"The Lord called me from the womb. From the body of my mother He named me."
(Isaiah 49:1)

Thank you for your love, prayers, phone calls, meals, flowers, food baskets and for being here today.

"No man is a failure who has friends."

That is a quote from the movie, "It's A Wonderful Life. "You have proven that our Dad is a success because of your friendship. I have watched you come to the hospital, hold his hand, kiss his forehead and touch his heart. I have seen you grieve as you saw his pain. I have listened to you laugh as you joyfully told us wonderful stories of his life. You have loved him well, and from what we have seen, he loved you well too.

Killen True Value was a source of life for him. Thank you Dan and Chris for believing in him. It didn't matter if he was sick or if his legs ached, he wanted to go to work. You have told us how he began every day with a smile, and how you could hear him laugh from the back of the store to the front. All of his coworkers were important to him.

Some of his favorite places were Hardee's, (he had to have his sausage and biscuits with gravy and some hot coffee), Killen Diner and Wal-Mart. His favorite place was home. He would sit on the front porch swing or in the livingroom and enjoy just being home. Thanks Donald. All of you are his people and you made this place full of life for him.

Dad loved running the roads to Nashville. He has seven grandchildren there. There were birthday parties, holidays, high school graduations and a wedding to celebrate with them. They loved their Paw Paw.

As we all know, Dad spent hours of his life in front of the mirror fixing his hair. He would rather do without a haircut than not go to BH Parker, his own barber. If he would have bought stock in Vita E hair spray, he would have been a wealthy man today.

The cancer may have taken his body, but it did not take his life because we carry his life in us every time we remember his smile, his laugh or his voice. He is a part of each of us. That is why we are here grieving his death and celebrating his life. So the next time you have a Little Debbie cake or Nutty Buddy bar or sausage biscuit, or listen to George Jones' songs know that Dad is smiling on you.

Dad carried his little Bible in his shirt pocket and read it every day. He said many times, "I love Jesus with all my heart." I know he did. I was thinking about who Jesus is and what He has done for Dad. I would like to share some of those things with you.

Jesus came to turn the hearts of the fathers to the children and the hearts children to their fathers. Our family is living proof of that truth. Jesus came to forgive ours sins and take them away. He came to give us eternal life. Jesus also came to take away the guilt of our sins. Our dad lived many years in guilt and shame and regret because of the choices he made. Many of you helped him through those years.

Almost five years ago he made a choice that changed his life. He stopped drinking and smoking. He said, "The good Lord helped me. It is all because of Him I'm sober. I give the man upstairs all the credit." Every year on the anniversary of that day, he bought himself a cake and put a candle on it to celebrate the miracle of his life without alcohol.

His story reminds me of this story in the Bible.

"I love you, O Lord, my strength. The Lord is my rock and my fortress and my deliverer. My God, my rock, in whom I take refuge. My shield and my salvation, my stronghold. I call upon the Lord who is worthy to be praised, and I am saved from my enemies. The cords of death surrounded me; the torrents of ungodliness terrified me. The cords of hell surrounded me; and the snares of death confronted me. In my distress I called upon the Lord and cried to my God for help. He heard my voice out of His temple, and my cry for help came into His ears. Then the earth shook and quaked and the foundations of the mountains were trembling and were shaken. He bowed the heavens also and came down. He delivered me from my strong enemy and from those who hated me, for they were too mighty for me. The Lord was my help. He rescued me because He delighted in me." (Psalm 18:1-9, 16-19)

And my favorite scripture:

"I acknowledged my sin to You, and my iniquity I did not hide. I said, 'I will confess my transgressions to the Lord.' And You forgave the guilt of my sin!"
(Psalm 32:5)

I want to share this scripture also. "The Lord is near to the broken-hearted and saves those who are crushed in spirit."
(Psalm 34:18)

We are broken-hearted today. We will miss picking up the phone to call him. We will miss going to his home to see him, or meeting him at a restaurant to eat with him. The pain is real. The Lord's presence to comfort you is real too. We will miss him greatly.

Here is a song that has helped me and my family through this:

"Cry Out to Jesus"

"For everyone who has lost someone they love
Long before it was their time
You feel like the days you had were not enough
When you said goodbye
And for all of the people with burdens and pains
Keeping you back from your life

You believe that there's nothing and there is no
one who can make it right

There is hope for the helpless, rest for the weary
Love for the broken heart
There is grace and forgiveness, mercy and healing
He'll meet you wherever you are
Cry out to Jesus"

Mac Powell/ Brad Avery/David Carr/ Tai Anderson/
Mark Lee/ Consuming Fire Music

Our family's prayer, and I know it would be Dad's prayer too, is for you to know this gracious and loving Jesus. For you to be able to say, "The good Lord helped me and it's all because of Him." And He can take away the guilt of your sin too. Then, we can all be together in Heaven, sitting around a big table laughing and eating biscuits and gravy with Dad. Who knows, maybe George Jones will sing for us too!

Here are few of my journal entries during this time while I was in Alabama.

January 1, 2006

I have been praying to value life more. I will miss my dad. He was enjoying working, having his own place to live, eating out, having money and being independent. It is sad to watch his health deteriorate so quickly. I pray for mercy over him. Lord have mercy!

January 4, 2006

I am grateful for eternal life; that when life ends here it doesn't end for our spirits. I grieve and feel like it is too soon to let dad go. I see him and his frailness and see his future of being incapable of taking care of himself, and I know how hard that would be for him. I ask God to keep the death angel away until the rest of the family can get here.

I pray for a strong heart and a strong mind and a soft countenance for myself. I pray that dad does not die alone. Freida's prayer is a good one; that God would take away the fear and terror from dad. The Lord showed me angels in the hospital room. God is good. I am torn between going home to Nashville and seeing Celeste back off to college and staying here until Nolan gets here tomorrow. Freida will be here Thursday. I can come back Sunday. I don't know, it could be days or weeks before dad goes to heaven. So many people have told me how special dad is to them.

I have a blessed life! I have a wonderful husband, three wonderful daughters, a wonderful son in law. It is a good life and I want to live it. Charity is safely in Greece. She sounds so good and excited. It is amazing how so much life can be going on in the middle of death. I don't want to miss out on living as I grieve dad's dying.

January 7, 2006

Bethany's birthday! She is so precious and wants to have fun in life. She is 22 years old, my age when I had her. I am home for the evening to give her a surprise birthday party!

January 8, 2006

I am grateful for a good day in the Lord. I prayed and meditated on God's goodness. I grieved and wailed over Dad's sickness. I danced and rejoiced over a good life. I talked with Celeste and Charity and Bethany and Ben and David. Then I went back to Alabama.

Tuesday, January 10, 2006

The cancer may have his body for a brief moment, but it won't have his life. Jesus will save dad from the effects of sin and cancer and heart problems. Dad keeps calling my name and I feel so helpless. Sometimes, I can't understand him at all and I have to guess at what he wants. I prayed over him. I told him he is a good dad and a good man. I prayed for God to be merciful and gracious to Dad, me, Freida, Davy, Nolan and all those who love him. He has a good name around here.

I had a good night's rest at Johnnie and Red's house. They know my story, history and background. They talked with Freida and me until 11 p.m. last night. They cooked us breakfast and talked with us today. They said that they are proud of Freida and me for following the Lord. And that it is a miracle we turned out the way we did.

It is so hard to not be able to hear dad or understand him. I can only offer cold water, cold washcloths and help adjust him in the hospital bed. I sit here and pray over him and bless him. I pray for God to take him with dignity and without fear. Part of me wants to be here when he dies and hold his hand. The other part of me is afraid to watch him take his last breath. Dad said, "It won't be long now. It won't be long now." At 4:30 p.m. today. Yesterday he said, "Rita, you have to get me out of here. I have to go home. I can't stay here alone." I asked him if he meant home to his house or home to Nashville. He said home to his house. I don't even think he meant his house. I think he meant Heaven. He hasn't been very alert today, but he still knows Freida and me and still recognizes people.

January 12, 2006

Dad has been in a lot of pain. He prayed, "O, Lord. O, my Lord." I am glad that Jesus is his Lord.

January 13, 2006

I am grateful for life, rest, people who pray for me, the love of God and the Word of God I have felt very alone. I surrender my hurt and disappointment. I heard the storm this morning and prayed for dad. He is so afraid of storms. I was going to rush to the hospital to be there so he wouldn't be alone. I realized that God is the only one who helps our aloneness and comforts us in our fears.

January 14, 2006

Here I sit watching him breathe heavily. He's going home from the hospital today. I believe he is going home to heaven soon. I pray for his home going to be smooth and without much pain. I really don't mind being here with him alone. Dave and Freida went to his house to get everything ready. I feel so helpless that I can't understand him. He tries so hard to get the words out. He is still trying to be independent. He puts his own chapstick on and suctions his congestion out of his mouth with the suction cup. He hates the catheter and still thinks he is strong enough to walk to the bathroom. I bent down to listen to him today and he kissed my face. There weren't enough hugs and kisses-given or received. The Eric Clapton song "No Tears In Heaven" speaks to me today.

I want to cry and scream and grieve, but this moment is not the time. I will be strong in the Lord and in His mighty power. Yes, I have cried and I will again, just not now. Dad wanted me to ride in the ambulance with him, but they wouldn't let me. Dad kept saying, "Don't leave me alone. Don't leave me alone." I told him I would be in my car right behind him. I cried all the way to his house. The lady from hospice set up the hospital bed in the living room. She told us to call if we needed anything. Many friends and family brought food. We felt very loved and cared for.

January 15, 2006

Well, Dad is in Heaven. He took his last breath here at 4:15 p.m. today. It was peaceful. He didn't struggle. I held one hand and Freida held the other. Vonda, Virginia, Marilyn, Kevin, Margaret, Jimbo, Shelia, Joan, Freida, Davy and I were there. Freida and I said a blessing over him. I kissed him and hugged him and listened to him take his last breath and then put my head on his chest to hear his last heartbeat. I can't believe how much I miss him already.

January 16, 2006

Killen True Value put yellow ribbons on the front doors today to honor my dad. I cried. Donald came over to tell us that it was an honor to have dad as a friend.

January 18, 2006

I didn't write at all yesterday. I was all talked out. The funeral was very honoring to God and to dad. People were given hope and comfort because of the Lord's presence. I spoke and was not nervous. I cannot quit crying. I knelt on the kitchen floor and wept. I cried out to Jesus. I am grieving not only for myself but for all of the dear friends that dad has who are missing him greatly. Charles and Betty Clark and Roxanne came to the funeral. Johnnie and Red, Gerald and Tracey and Brother Williams as well as many, many others came too. It touched my heart so much to have people from my childhood and teenage years there.

Norma Charlene Robinson Phillips
3/09/1937-- 5/25/1999

My mom was born in Molus, Kentucky on March 9, 1937. She had seven brothers and sisters. One of her older sisters died as a child. Mom grew up going to church and believing in God. She wasn't taught that God was very loving or caring. She had a very strict mother. She grew up in the hills of Kentucky. Life was hard for her and her family. Her dad left when she was a teenager. She was 13 or 14 when she moved to Chicago with her mom and younger sister, Willa. She quit school in the 8th grade and started working. She looked much older than she was and she was a good worker. My mother grew up fast and had a lot of responsibility. She loved to laugh and joke around and had good friends.

She married my dad when she was 22 years old in 1959. They had a rocky marriage from the start. They loved each other, yet didn't know how to get along. They divorced in 1976, after many separations. Her heart was broken and so was her spirit. She didn't believe in divorce, but there were no other options.

She was a strict mother too. When she found herself raising four children as a single mom, she was very afraid. Because she was so mature and responsible at a young age, she expected the same from us. She loved God and wanted to please Him. She was afraid of never measuring up to the belief system she had that God wanted her to be perfect. She lived a lonely life inside. I loved watching her pray and sing at church. That seemed to be the only place that she was free.

Mom loved babies: baby children, baby kittens, baby puppies, baby goats. We would take our three girls to see her in Kentucky and she would have a litter of kittens or puppies waiting for them. She had a litter of preemie kittens that our girls got to feed with baby bottles. Oh, what fun that was for them. She would drive them around her rural Kentucky town and show them the baby cows and baby sheep. I believe there was a part of her innermost being that missed out on being treated like a baby or a little child when she was young. She loved holding my girls when they were babies and wrapping them in blankets and cuddling them until they fell asleep.

She moved to Alabama from Kentucky. She was diagnosed with cancer in January of 1999. I went to Alabama to go to the doctor with her. The doctor said the cancer was incurable and that she had a year to live. He wanted to give her radiation for the pain. I watched her face as she received the news. She became very brave and asked what she should do next. I so appreciate what the doctor told her. He told her to live the next months instead of focusing on dying. He told her to go to Nashville and see her granddaughter get baptized. He told her to make sure everything was in order for her life. Then we walked out of the doctor's office in silence.

I believe that God heals our physical bodies as well as our souls. Mom said that she did not want to be healed here on earth. She said that she wanted to go on to heaven, that her time here was through. I went home to Nashville and left her in Alabama. That is what she wanted. I drove back to Alabama a week later to take her to her first radiation treatment and follow- up doctor's visit. I had to help her go to the bathroom and help her get out of the shower. She fought for every ounce of independence she could. After all, she had been on her own for so long, and being independent is all she knew. I would like to share with you a few journal entries from her time before she went to be with the Lord. Please, know that I love my Mom and I am grateful that she is the mother that God blessed me with here on earth.

April 19, 1999

Here I sit at ECM Hospital coffee shop as mom is getting a radiation treatment. She isn't doing too well. It probably won't be long until she will need a wheelchair and more care. I hate to see her suffer. Her back, leg, and head hurt. The cancer is in several places and in some of her bones.

May 1, 1999

Mom came to Nashville to watch Emily get baptized. The doctor told her to come. I am glad that she came. A day or so later she started feeling out of control pain. Mom is in the hospital. She went in Thursday, April 29. She was in a lot of pain. She has been so cruel with her words. I love her and grieve for her, but it still hurts.

May 7, 1999

Here I am at the hospital listening to mom wheeze as she breathes. She is not completely coherent today. She hates feeling this way. When I came in at 7:30 a.m. she was in uncontrollable pain. She was vicious and physically out of control. She had already torn out two IV's. She was threatening to hit me. She was mean to the nurse too. The neurologist said that it was not the medicine or the pain talking but that it was her personality disorder. He told me to not stay too long or talk too much, that it doesn't help her or the family. She still knows who we are, thankfully.

I don't have dates for the following thoughts, but these are the ones I had during that time. I bought mom a birthday card March 9. I knew that it would be her last birthday here on earth. I bought her a night light that was her favorite, two children walking across a wooden bridge with an angel watching over them. It was hard for me to buy anything because I knew that it would be coming back to me soon. For Mother's Day I went to the store to buy her a card. I stood there and cried. I couldn't buy one. I knew that she was dying and that the card would eventually be mine too.

I went to an Ann Graham Lotz conference and received some healing for my emotions. After the conference I went back to the hospital. It was about 10 p.m. I sat in mom's room and read the Bible to her. I told her that I loved her and that I was glad that she was my mom. I thanked her for all the sacrifices she made for me to have food and shelter. I thanked her for taking me to church and telling me about Jesus. I blessed her and prayed over her. Then I sat there and cried. I finally went home with peace.

After that I still went to the hospital every day. I did not spend the night there though. Part of me was afraid. I just couldn't watch her die. I wanted to remember her alive. Mom went to be with the Lord in the early hours of the morning of May 25, 1999. I wrote and gave a eulogy for her service. I wore a yellow dress instead of black. I wasn't being disrespectful; I definitely was grieving. But I wanted to celebrate her life in Heaven. She was finally free. She had so longed to go be with Jesus. She wanted her heart to be free and her body to quit hurting. I was so glad for her to be celebrating seeing Jesus! I knew that I would see her again. That is the promise Jesus made when He gave us eternal life.

One of the songs that she sang at church comes to my mind right now.

> *"I have found His grace is all complete*
> *He supplieth every need*
> *While I sit and learn at Jesus' feet*
> *I am free, yes free indeed*
> *It is joy unspeakable and full of glory*
> *Oh, the half has never yet been told."*

Sing on, Mom. I'll be up there to sing with you one day!

At the Cross

I am yearning for companionship with God, that is why I come to the Abbey of Gethsemani every year. My broken life is healed by Christ's brokenness for me. I walk to the cross as my first venture out of my room. The cross is across the street and up a steep hill. At this cross I have cried and laughed. I have told God my deepest desire, my greatest shame, my biggest fears and my loftiest dreams.

On my first trip here, about six years ago, I went to the cross. I quietly walked up to the base of it. The cross is about three feet up on a hill on some rocks. I prayed silently and reverently. I shed a few tears and started to walk down the hill. As I was walking, a boy about six years old was running up the hill with his parents behind him. He ran up to the cross, climbed up the rocks and grabbed onto the foot of the cross. He started swinging around and threw his paper airplane at his parents. He laughed and had fun. I stood there watching this young boy in his innocence and freedom. He got it! Freedom at the cross. Life at the cross.

So much of my life has been spent in following Christ in the fellowship of His sufferings that I forget to walk with Him in the power of His resurrection. I got a little jealous of this boy's freedom. I walked down the trail and kept the cross in view. As soon as the child and his parents left, I ran back up the hill to the cross. I climbed the rocks, grabbed onto the cross and cried loudly. Then I laughed awhile. Then I just sat there breathing in God's pleasure. I got it! Freedom at the cross. Life at the cross. God delights in me no matter what condition I am in when I come to the cross. He is just glad when I come. I believe that life is good because of the cross.

I have been to the cross and put flowers there representing my husband, each of my children, my son-in-law and myself. I put them there right after I get here. We are all at the foot of the cross where grace and suffering meet. I have to put all of us at the feet of Jesus so that I don't try to carry our burdens. When I start to wonder how they are during the few days I am here, I remember that Jesus is taking care of them.

Since this is a time to get away from the noise and clutter and busyness of life, I try to only check my cell phone messages once a day. So far, I have succeeded at checking them twice a day. I have called my husband and children too. The only place I can get good clear reception is at the top of the hill by the cross. I believe that is symbolic of how I need to live my life. The only good and clear communication I can have with anyone is through Jesus.

There, at the cross, I have compassion for people who are hurting, grace for people who are failing, and wisdom for those who need guidance.

The Woods Path

Across the street from the Abbey there are two trails going up to the statues of the Apostles and Jesus in the garden of Gethsemani. One of them is the Woods Path and the other is the Open Field Path. There is a large pond and several foot trails. As I was walking along the Woods Path I saw a tree that had a big trunk; it splits and comes back together at the top. The sign on the tree says, "This tree splits at the bottom and reunites at the top." I looked at that tree and thought of my life. I was born in one piece and then split. I never felt whole while I was growing up.

There always seemed to be two worlds going on when I was a child and teenager. We went to church on Sunday and prayed and sang and dressed nicely. Not very many people knew that during the week there was fighting and drinking and total chaos at our house. I had to keep the family secret, and my heart was being torn in pieces.

As I looked at that tree I grieved. I wept until I couldn't cry anymore. Then I breathed in the grace of God to heal the past wounds. The Lord was with me during those crazy times growing up. It was not until I was in my 30s that I finally came back together. Now, I am one with God and myself again.

I reached the garden and looked at the life-size statues of the disciples sleeping in the garden. I thought of how many times I have been sleepy when Jesus asked me to pray. The next scene in the garden is Jesus on His knees praying to the Father. This is a life-size statue also. Jesus has His hands on His face praying in deep agony. Jesus praying. Jesus, Son of God, praying to His Father. I wept and hung onto Jesus' arms. I thanked Him for going through the pain and torment to redeem me. I heard myself saying, "I am not a failure. I am not a failure. I am not a failure!"

For much of my life I had felt like I was a failure. It was while I was holding onto Jesus that I realized that He did not view me as a failure. He redeemed me from all my sins and failures- past and present. Then I realized the prayer that Jesus was praying was for me to become one of His children. Me holding on to Jesus and Him holding on to me!

The Meadow

On one of my walks I ventured out into a vast meadow. I wasn't sure if I was allowed to go or not. There was no one to ask, so I did it anyway. I laid out in the field in the sunshine. I find that I am adventurous and inquisitive and like to get off the marked path. I went back to my room to shower before going to bed. Then I realized that I had brought some living things back to the room with me. I had ticks all over me! After a quiet scream (after all the Abbey is a place of silence), I started picking ticks off of me. That night I dreamed that I had ticks crawling on me. I woke up and checked again. I was checking for ticks for days!

I don't believe that I was being punished for getting off the path. I was suffering the consequences for being foolish and sitting in the eight-inch-tall grass in April. Excuse me for a moment; I have to go do a tick check now. I think I feel something crawling on me.

As I was going back to the Retreat House, I saw a beer bottle in the grass. Someone had thrown it from a car. I know that the monks are responsible for keeping the grounds clean and I wanted to be of service, so I bent down and picked it up. I looked for a trash can on the property. None. I looked for a trash can outside the Retreat House. None. Here I was, coming from fervent prayer at the cross, carrying an empty beer bottle into the Abbey Retreat House. Oh great, I did find a trash can inside the building in the front room where the priest signs in the guests. A lesson on humility for me.

Open Field Path

On a different trip to the Abbey I walked up to the garden of Gethsemani to see the statues. I took the Open Field Path because the Woods Path was overgrown and a little scary to me. I wore jeans, socks, athletic shoes, and a lightweight jacket with a hood over my head. Did I mention that it was June 4th and 90 degrees outside?

Father Christian said to be careful because most of the woods are overgrown and the ticks are everywhere. From past experience, I was not taking any chances on tick infestation. After covering myself completely, I sprayed my shoes, socks, jeans and hands with "Off" bug spray. If I hadn't been afraid of having an allergic reaction, I honestly would have sprayed my face too. I figured that if I had the hood tied tightly around my chin and eyes that ticks couldn't possibly get on my face. I set off on my walk to see and hear God. I knew that He was waiting for me.

After shooing off some flies and looking for snakes, I settled into a brisk walking pace. As I got closer the grass got high and the trees in the woods became more dense. My heart was beating a little faster too. It wasn't from fear or from the walk. I knew that I was getting closer to meeting with Jesus.

He has met me in that garden every time I go. It isn't just because of the life-sized statues either. It is what those statues represent to me. As I walked up to the sleeping disciples statues, I reflected on how they must have felt that day in the real garden. They were tired, not fully aware of what was about to happen and so human. Then I walked up the trail to the life-sized statue of Jesus. I stood and looked and prayed.

"Wholeness"

Wholeness is the word the Lord breathed to me through the trees. "Rita, you are whole! You don't have to look any longer. You are whole!" I leaned into His voice and said, "Yes, I receive Your gift of wholeness." Then I walked up the trail to the empty cross. I needed to see the empty cross. The crucifixion would have been in vain if Jesus had not come off the cross and out of the tomb. I needed to know that Jesus' life and death were not in vain. I already knew the outcome of the story. I know that He was crucified, dead, buried, then resurrected and ascended to the right hand of the Father. I know that with all my heart. And with all my heart today, I needed to be reminded of it.

"Freedom"

Freedom is the word the Lord whispered in the wind. I leaned into the wind and heard it again. "Freedom!" Yes, that is it! I get it! If Jesus prayed for me to be whole in the Garden of Gethsemani, that means He purchased my freedom and wholeness when He died on the cross! When He said, "It is finished!" He meant it.

I knelt at the cross and cried with gratitude for awhile. I saw two medium sized rocks at the cross. I picked one up and realized that it represented the stony place in my heart. I have prayed before for my heart to be softened and it has been. Today though, there was a supernatural exchange happening in my heart.

You see, before the walk I had completed the chapters in this book about my mom and dad. I found closure concerning their lives and deaths and shared it with you. I spoke of them with love and compassion and dignity. It has taken years of healing and prayer to see them through Jesus' eyes. I wanted to blame them for the hardships in my life. God has taken that out of my heart completely. Today, I know that they are whole and free too. I am glad that I don't have to wait until I get to Heaven to hear, "Rita, you are whole and free!" They loved the Lord here on earth too.

The scripture that the Lord brings to my mind right now is Ezekiel 11:19:

> *"And I shall give them one heart, and put a new spirit within them. And I will take the heart of stone out of their flesh and give them a heart of flesh, that they will walk in my statutes and keep my ordinances and do them. Then they will be My people and I will be their God."*

The other rock at the cross represented the rocks that I keep in my hands to throw at people who hurt me. I secretly keep one close at all times in case I feel attacked or misunderstood or mistreated. It is hard to admit that. I realize that is what I am doing every time someone disagrees with me and I talk about them. Or, if you hurt me first, I have my rock ready to throw at you behind your back. Ugly, isn't it?

I picked up both rocks and held them up to the sky and cried out for forgiveness. I needed forgiveness for every person I have held hostage in my heart for disappointing me, not seeing me and not helping me when I needed help. I received God's great mercy there at the cross. I held onto those rocks and wept. I felt my heart beat through my chest. I felt God's heartbeat too. Whew, forgiveness- to receive it and give it. What an amazing miracle. The rocks are there at the cross. I left them there. I don't have use for them anymore. I look at my hands and they are free. I looked at my heart and it is free. Yes, whole and free!

My daughter Bethany summed it up well in this song she wrote when she was seventeen:

At The Cross

"Holy abandon, passionate grace
Flowing along with the blood from Your face
Seen from a distance, looked on with fear
Ultimate sacrifice to draw us near

At the cross lies the hope of the world
At the cross where dreams lay unfurled
At the cross is the victory won
Life does not end it's begun
At the cross

Seemed like a failure all hope was lost
Death cried triumphantly 'Where is your God?'
The whole earth was shaken with no one to save
When out of the darkness You conquered the grave!

At the cross lies the hope of the world
At the cross where dreams lay unfurled
At the cross is the victory won
Life does not end it's begun
At the cross"

Bethany Nicholson/ Glory Alleluia Music/ ASCAP

Some Eulogies

Eulogy: a speech or writing in praise of a person.

We usually hear eulogies at funerals. Others can hear the wonderful words being spoken, but the deceased can't hear those words. Usually the eulogy describes how we love, respect and admire the person. Here are some people who have been a part of my life. Some have gone on to be with the Lord and some are here on this earth. They are all in my heart. I am forever grateful for the part that each person played in my life.

Grandma: I was told that you stayed in the hospital with me when I was about two years old. I had a fever of 105 degrees for a week. You also called me your little angel. I needed to feel like I was special to someone. Thank you! I love you! See you in Heaven. We can eat fried okra and fried potatoes and strawberry cake when I get there!

The Preacher at the storefront Pentecostal Church in Chicago: For letting me play the tambourine at the services when I was a young child. I was making music for the Lord even though I was making noise to everyone else. I wish I knew your name. I am sure that God does! Thanks.

The Presbyterian Children's Church leaders in Tuscumbia, AL: For feeding me on Sunday nights (you didn't know that we didn't have much food at our house). For teaching me the song "Onward Christian Soldiers." For making the Bible stories come to life on the flannelgraph board. Thanks.

The church bus driver taking us to the Missionary Baptist Church in Florence, AL: For the candy and gum and fun. I loved going to church and you provided that blessing to this little girl. Thanks.

The Church of God of Prophecy in Sheffield, AL: Oh my, where do I begin? All of you, for Christmas presents, food, fellowship, prayers every Sunday night at the altar, acceptance, teaching. Only God knows how you saved this girl's life by loving me. Thanks.

Charles Clark, owner of Muscle Shoals Kentucky Fried Chicken: For being a godly male authority figure in my life. You were one I could trust and look up to. For trusting me enough to let me borrow your van so I could take a bunch of youth to a retreat in Birmingham. For Christmas presents and bonuses. I worked for you through my teenage years and you were such a blessing. I appreciate you and Betty coming to see me when my dad died. It meant a lot to me. May God bless your sons to be like you! Thanks.

Mrs. Miller, my tenth grade College Prep. English teacher at Sheffield High School: For seeing through the grammar and content of my English papers and seeing the content of my heart. For keeping me after class and asking how I was doing when my parents were going through their divorce. For sending me a silver rose vase for my wedding. I still have it. For saying a prayer for me when I was scared. For writing a pass for me for my next class because I was going to be late because I stayed late after your class crying. For never making me feel stupid because I was scared. You should have a special jewel in your crown. I am sure that I was not the only teenage girl you helped. Thanks.

Mrs. Ikard - Sheffield High School Choir Teacher: I had you as my choir teacher 6th through 12th grades. You helped me learn how to stay on pitch and taught me how to read music. Thanks for encouraging me to try out for All State Choir. You gave me confidence in my singing and helped me to develop a love for it. Thanks for all the extra hours of practice after school and the fun choir trips all over the state of Alabama. Okay, they were fun for me. I hope you had some fun too. For believing in me. Thanks.

Pat Byrd, friend: For letting me live with you for a few months during a crisis point in my life. For giving me a special Bible. For praying with me and praying for me many, many times. For treating me like a daughter. Wherever you are, thanks.

Johnnie and Red - friends in Sheffield, AL: For coming to my house to pray when I was a teenager. For letting Freida and me stay at your home while Dad was in the hospital. For cooking for us. For staying up late and getting up early so we could have someone to talk to during my Dad's battle with cancer. For praying over us every morning before we went to the hospital.

For understanding where we came from, where we had been, and blessing us with your "well words." I am forever grateful. Thanks.

Roxanne Walker - forever friend: For all the years working together at KFC. For laughing, crying, fighting and praying together. For years of growing, through having children and watching them grow up. You are never far from my heart though you are in another state. I love you girl. Thanks.

Sue Turner McGray - Mary Kay Cosmetics National Sales Director: For spurring me on to become the best person I could be. For smiling at me all the time. For having a joyous spirit. For telling me not to pressure myself and to enjoy the journey. Journeying with you was fun. Thanks for letting me hold your meeting when you were out of town. I felt special. All God's best. Thanks.

Sue Johnson - beloved friend: Just writing your name makes me smile. Your love and enthusiasm for the Lord and life makes my heart sing. I want to be like you when I grow up. In the midst of my craziness you saw potential and asked me to be a Bible Study Leader! I was humbled and honored and so excited. You believed that I could do it, so I believed I could do it. You always made me feel like you were so proud of me. I needed that to the core of my being. I loved serving the Lord with you in BSF. You taught me much. I love, love, love you! Thanks.

Barbi White - friend of God: For your countless hours of counsel. For holding me accountable to seek truth. For showing me grace in that accountability. For having the Beloved Women group at your house. For teaching me how to cry through the pain and heal through the pain. For sharing your life and story with me. For helping me to not hate myself. For showing me the love of God. You will know when you get to heaven how you helped me. I love your passion and honesty. I love you with my heart! Thanks.

Rozan McDaniel - friend and sister (by heart): For walking this road of life with me. For having a good name so I could name my firstborn after you. For sharing your sons with me. For helping me to laugh at myself. For traveling this life with me both literally and spiritually.

For gifts and offerings and love. You are a part of my life forever. Thanks.

Debbie Lynn Pugh: For letting me name my firstborn twin after you. For your great laugh. For letting me in to be a part of your life. For you being a part of my life. For letting your kids be our godkids. For staying close when I couldn't find myself. For knowing where Cumberland and Totz, KY are. There is a tie that keeps us connected. Thanks.

Melinda Ols - heart to heart friend: For showing me how to be a good friend by being a good friend. Your perseverance and tenacity spur me on to be the best me. Your passion to live by truth and love motivate me. You are a good mom. You amaze me! Thanks.

Alice Greene - tea drinking friend: For getting together with me and letting me brag on my kids. For listening to my problems and for helping me see that they weren't problems after all. For sharing your heart and life with me. I count that as a great privilege. You are beautiful inside and out. Thanks.

Becky Peacock - my newest forever friend: For having me and David in your home before you knew us. For cooking gluten-free food for me that was delicious. For letting Jesus shine through your whole countenance. For the godly example you are to your husband, children and church friends. You are truly a servant of Christ.

Looking forward to many years of a growing friendship with you. God knew Kuwait needs a woman of passion like you. I am blessed to know you. Thanks.

Patricia Cross - Beloved Woman of God: You've seen me at my best and worst. You call. You listen. You trust. You believe in the good in me and you bring the good out of me! Oh, I can't wait to dance together when we get to heaven! I love you dearly. Thanks.

Priscilla Craig - sweet friend: You have been an example of humility, strength in weakness, and healing. Your love of life gives me energy. I love you! Thanks.

Rhonda Rush - Friend: Your tenacity to follow Jesus and be whole blesses my heart! I love you and I'm glad that we are true friends! Thanks.

Freida - my sister: Your desire to live life and pursue God inspires me. We have walked most of this journey together. I know that telling my story also tells some of yours. I am glad that God chose you to be my sister. Life would not have been as rich without you. (After all, you helped me bake the bird, and you could have told someone I was in the locker). You know where Totz is. We can laugh now. God is the Redeemer. Oh, I love you from the bottom of my heart! Thanks.

Emily Diane - beautiful grown niece: You are full of grace and beauty. God delights in you and has so much blessing for your life. I am so blessed to have you as my niece! I love you.

Maximus, Isabella and Penelope - the cutest nephew and nieces on earth: Just watching you live life gives joy to my heart! To hear you laugh. To watch your tee ball and soccer games. I love you more than I can find words for! Thanks for letting me read Cat in the Hat to you!

Dudley Hall - favorite minister: for helping me grasp the Word of God. For showing me God's grace in living life. For having fun and enjoying the journey! Thanks.

Laura Nicholson - lovely lady of God: you are an inspiration to your generation! Your passion and heart for the Lord is so obvious. Jesus is your first love. I am glad to have you in my life and in our family. Love you much.

Lynn Taff - prayer warrior friend: you are tenacious, gracious and full of life and love! I appreciate walking this journey of life with you. You are a great blessing to my heart.

Mike and Loretta Hopkins: you are two of my favorite people that God created! I love your heart for Jesus and for His creation and His children. I have learned much from you. Thanks for living in Italy so we can come there and minister with you! Love you.

Mercy Refused

"Justice demanded satisfaction
The law had been broken again and again.
Judgment required immediate action
Death wanted payment for sin.
But Mercy refused and Love took my place
There on a cross where Justice met Grace
Mercy refused to let me die
Jesus the Lamb was crucified.
Though rightfully, Death wanted me; Mercy refused

Christ has become my righteousness.
The Lord is my peace and my freedom from sin.
Now I am clothed in His holiness
To a new life I entered in.
When Mercy refused and Love took my place
There on a cross where Justice met Grace
Mercy refused to let me die
Jesus the Lamb was crucified
Though rightfully, Death wanted me; Mercy refused

As far as the Heavens are over the earth
So great is His mercy to us!
As far as the east is from the west
That's how far He's removed our transgressions from us!

When Mercy refused and Love took our place.
There on a cross where Justice met Grace
Mercy refused to let us die
Jesus the Lamb was crucified
Though rightfully, Death wanted you and me
Mercy refused."

I have always loved that song written by my husband. 1999 was a year that I clung to the mercy of the Lord for dear life. My mom was diagnosed with cancer in January. I was in the doctor's office with her. I saw fear and resolve. She always tried to be so brave and strong. I am sure the doctor saw the same thing in my face, fear and resolve. Part of me had to be strong that day for Mom. Part of me was tired of being strong. I was lonely and afraid. Afraid of what the future would hold for her (and me). I was also angry. Very angry.

Angry that Mom would not see her grandchildren grow up. Angry that I had never felt accepted or really loved by her. I was angry with God at the seeming injustice of it all. I was a desperate woman who loved God and wanted to please Him. I was a woman who was desperate to feel protected and nurtured and cared for.

Apparently, in my wounded frame of mind, I did not feel like God was doing a good job of taking care of me. In my desperation and rebellion I had an affair. I was devastated at my actions. My heart was being torn. I was going against everything I believed in. I knew that one day I would have to tell my husband and children. I wanted to die, but I couldn't. I was taking care of mom in the hospital. I had three daughters to love. I had a husband to reconcile with. Living would be harder than dying for me at that time.

I confided in a godly counselor who helped me to repent and start to reconcile with God, myself and my husband. She gave me wisdom and guidance and grace. She was a fragrance of grace to me.

I told David and watched his heart break. We were in couples' counseling for a long time. He forgave me and stayed with me. I begged God not to let my sins be passed on to my daughters. I prayed for them all the time. When they were older, after prayer, counsel, and in agreement with David, I told each of my girls individually. They responded with love and forgiveness. I was amazed at their maturity and their ability to be a fragrance of grace to me.

I have shared my story with people whom the Lord has told me to. I have a group of women with whom I meet weekly. The woman at the well knew what I felt: guilt, shame and isolation. When she met Jesus she received His grace and mercy. She told everyone.

I have waited over nine years to tell my story publicly. I wondered if I would ever be qualified to minister again. I wondered if God would trust me with His Word. I wondered if I could truly accept grace and mercy and forgiveness. I wondered if my marriage would ever be whole. The answer to all those questions is YES. I am qualified. God trusts me. My marriage is restored and whole.

The first time I received communion after I received God's forgiveness, I truly understood the scripture in Romans 5:20, 21. *"Where sin abounded, grace much more abounded. So that as sin reigned in death, even so grace reigned through righteousness to eternal life through Jesus Christ our Lord."*

My sin was covered by grace. Jesus' grace. As I am writing now, my heart is beating a little fast. I am hoping that you will accept me. I am trusting that the fragrance of God's grace is coming through these words to your heart. *"Though rightfully, death wanted me; Mercy refused."*

Bethany and I ministered together at a Ladies' Retreat not long ago. The Women's Minister of that church knows my story and said that it would be fine for me to share it. I did not plan on sharing my whole story that day but Bethany encouraged me to share deeply, and to speak what God wanted me to. After lunch, Bethany led worship and spoke on Thankfulness. It was so good and powerful. The women loved having her there. I was to finish the day by sharing for a few moments and then sing "Mercy Refused."

As I was talking about Legion in Luke 8, I felt like I should tell my whole story. Legion knew what it was like to be alone, tormented, living among the dead, ashamed, and naked. No one could help him. He cried out and hurt himself day and night. Then Jesus comes to him and says ,"What is your name?" He looks into Legion's heart and sees who he really is- a person needing to be saved from himself. Jesus delivers him from the tormenting spirits. Then we see Legion clothed and in his right mind, sitting at the feet of Jesus. Legion begs to go with Jesus, but he is told to go back home to his family and friends, and to tell them what Jesus had done for him.

So, that is what I am doing. I am telling you and everyone who wants to listen what Jesus has done for me. I am not naked and ashamed anymore. I am not living among the dead anymore. I am clothed and in my right mind, ever at the feet of Jesus worshiping him for bringing me back to life!

"Grace to you and peace from God our Father and the Lord Jesus Christ. Blessed be the God and Father of our Lord Jesus Christ, who has blessed us with every spiritual blessing in the heavenly places in Christ. Just as He chose us in Him before the foundation of the world. That we would be holy and blameless before Him. In love He predestined us to adoption as sons through Jesus Christ to Himself, according to the kind intention of His will. To the

praise of the glory of His grace which He freely
bestowed on us in the beloved. In Him we have
redemption through His blood, the forgiveness of sins
according to the riches of His grace."
(Ephesians 1:2-7)

I Hope You Dance

When I was a little girl I would put on a skirt and twirl around until I was dizzy. "I am a dancer!" I would say. As I grew older, dreams got pushed aside for the reality of life. I forgot to keep dancing. Then I forgot how to dance.

As a teenager in the late 1970's, the "electric slide" dance became popular. I was really good at that dance. It was a pretty basic dance with 4 counts. 1-2-3-4, turn; 1-2-3-4, turn. It was fun but not very interesting and no room for individual creativity. The whole crowd got on the dance floor; we all did the 4 steps and turned at the same time. We would add a little hip movement or shoulder movement. But we all ended up turning at the same time and counting to 4. It was symbolic of how my life was. Don't make up any moves of my own. Do life choreographed by someone else. Follow the crowd. Don't get out of step. Stay in line with everyone. I wanted to break out of the line and dance my own dance but I wanted to fit in and be a part of the crowd too. So, I stayed with the choreographed dance.

Then I had three little girls who never stopped moving, jumping and dancing. I bought them dance costumes and dress up outfits and plastic high-heeled shoes. They twirled and laughed and made up their own dances. I put them in ballet classes when they were young. They loved the outfits and the shoes but not so much the classes themselves. We moved to another city and they played softball and took gymnastics. Then they took a few more dance classes. Basketball took up lots of time, but they never stopped dancing at home and with friends. Then we found a place that taught jazz and hip-hop dance. The girls were really good. They were so free when they danced. I would go to their dance competitions and cry as I watched them. It wasn't because I thought they were so good (though they were). There was something stirring inside my heart:

"The Dance."

Maybe I was remembering what it was like to be free and to dance for the love of dancing. I was longing for the unscripted and unchoreographed dance. The Lord of the Dance was drawing me to dance again.

I love the song *"I Hope You Dance"* sung by Leann Womack. The words are so powerful:

> *"I hope you never lose your sense of wonder*
> *Get your fill to eat but always keep that hunger*
> *May you never take one single breath for granted*
> *God forbid love ever leave you empty- handed*
> *I hope you still feel small*
> *When you stand beside the ocean*

Whenever one door closes I hope one more opens
Promise me that you'll give faith a fighting chance
When you get the choice to sit it out or dance...
I hope you dance. I hope you dance

I hope you never fear those mountains in the
distance
Never settle for the path of least resistance
Living might mean taking chances
But they're worth taking
Loving might be a mistake but it's worth making
Don't let some hellbent heart leave you bitter
When you come close to selling out- reconsider
Give the heavens above more than just a passing
glance
When you get the choice to sit it out or dance...
I hope you dance. I hope you dance"

Mark D. Sanders/ Tia Sillers/ MCA Music Publishing/ Soda Creek
Songs/Choice is Tragic Music Publishing/ Ensign Music/
BMI/ ASCAP

I sing that song in many church services because it tells of the heart of God for us to dance. Life does get hard sometimes and we forget to dance. Yet, God is always wooing us to come away with Him to dance the uninhibited dance.

When I go to The Abbey in Kentucky every year to slow down, calm down and quiet down; I can hear the

Dancer call to me in the hills and trees and flowers and creeks filled with water. On one of my walks I went into the vast open field and danced. As far as I could tell there was not anyone around. I sang:

"Dance with me, oh lover of my soul
To the song of all songs
Romance me, oh, lover of my soul
To the song of all songs"

(Chris DuPre/ Integrity's Hosanna Music/ ASCAP)

I twirled. I put my hand in dance partner position like there was someone dancing with me (He was). I laughed. And I danced. How good it felt. God and me. He was happy that I took Him up on the offer to be His dance partner.

I was at a conference in Denver, Colorado with my husband. We taught on worship and music and the love of God. At the end of my session on dancing and dreaming, I felt like having the congregation dance. I sang "I Hope You Dance." Then guess what I did? I taught them the "electric slide." Yes, right there on the platform of the church, in front of God and everybody. It was awesome. I believe that some of the people heard the wooing of the Lord of the Dance for the first time in awhile. *So, we danced!*

I still dance at home a lot. God loves it when I dance. Not because I am so good (though He thinks I am), but because freedom stirs in my heart when I dance. It's the unscripted and spontaneous dance of life.

All of my girls have danced and taught dance and still dance. They are the most fun to watch when the three of them are together. They have different styles and moves, yet they are amazing together. They are free when they dance. I still cry when I see them dance, not because they are so good (which they are), but because I see the Lord of the Dance in them-free and uninhibited and unchoreographed. So, when you get the choice to sit it out or dance...

I hope you dance!

"You have turned my sorrow into joyful dancing. No longer am I sad and wearing sackcloth. I thank you from my heart and I will never stop singing your praises, my Lord and my God!"
(Psalm 30:11, 12 CEV)

"You have turned for me my mourning into dancing! You have loosed my sackcloth and girded me with gladness! That my soul may sing praise to you and not be silent. O Lord my God, I will give thanks to you forever!"
(Psalm 30:11, 12 NASB)

Sovereign Grace

I see God's sovereignty throughout my life. He knew who my parents would be, where I would be born, who I would marry, how many children I would have. He knows the rest of my life too. He has chosen not to let me know what the future will be, but He has told me that He knows what my future will be. He is the great "I Am." He was with me in the past, with me in the now and will be with me in the future.

As I finish this book of remembrances and testimonies of God's faithfulness, I want to share what is going on in my life today. I am traveling and speaking at Women's Conferences and churches. I ministered in Kuwait for a Ladies' Conference. It was titled "I'm Living My Destiny!" Those wonderful women from many countries blessed me so much! I am singing more. I am traveling with David around the world and loving being a team with him.

David and I will celebrate 28 years of marriage on November 1, 2008. We will celebrate that day in Rome, Italy. (David is Italian, you know).We will also go to Vienna, Austria and Lugano, Switzerland. We have been privileged to become friends with some of the most amazing people who are giving their lives to serve Jesus and help others. We gratefully get to minister along side of them.

I am amazed at how this Chicago-Kentucky-Alabama girl gets to live this life. When I am home in Tennessee, I have wonderful friends and awesome family to love. I attend The Gate church in Franklin. I have community. I enjoy being at home and watching football games and going to movies with Bethany, Ben and Celeste. I am going to see Charity in Los Angeles soon. I go to my niece and nephew's soccer games.

I have received what I longed for my whole life… to belong.

Bethany, who is married to Ben, lives close by in Spring Hill, TN. They married on July 30, 2005. They have built their marriage on love, accountability and openness. I am amazed at their maturity. When they wanted to get married at 21 years of age, I knew that it would be okay because they are both teachable and willing to receive help. (No standing in the field throwing rocks at each other for their marriage).

They are amazing songwriters, worship leaders, worshipers, lovers of God and lovers of people. Bethany is in Bible School and works part time. She is a mentor to young women. Ben works full time and mentors young men and is a great guitar player and producer! We are thankful to have this Englishman in the family.

In God's sovereignty, He took Bethany from Tennessee and Ben from England and put them in Newcastle, Australia. They met while serving in a mission organization called Youth With a Mission. They worked with at-risk teens, telling them of the love of Jesus. They realized that they loved each other, and as the saying goes, "the rest is history." As they were giving those years of their lives to help others, God was making great plans for their lives. Their commitment to God and each other is a shining example for other couples.

Psalm 37:3,4 says:

"Trust in the Lord and do good. Dwell in the land and cultivate faithfulness. Delight yourself in the Lord and He will give you the desires of your heart."

Now I am waiting for some cute little Nicholson grandbabies that I can love and cuddle and spoil!

Charity Lynne is living in Los Angeles pursuing her dreams of being a dancer/singer. She has the giftings to be anything she wants. She has the tenacity to do it too. Her first few months in L.A. weren't easy. After being there 30 days she was in a car wreck and totalled her car. She had to get rides to work, which wasn't easy because she worked from 6 p.m. until 2 A.M. She had to move twice. She is strong and knows her purpose. She loves God and loves people. She has always loved to dance and sing and perform. Now she is waiting to show the world her talent.

She brings such joy to everyone who knows her. I miss her quite a lot. I will get to see her Thanksgiving - not soon enough. *"For I know the plans I have for you, declares the Lord; plans to prosper you, not to harm you, to give you a future and a hope."* Jeremiah 29:11 NASB

Celeste Gabrielle is living at home during her transition time. She lived in Athens, Greece teaching Kindergarten at Glyfada Christian Academy. She was there from August 2007 through June 2008. She misses all those beautiful European and Middle Eastern children. She is full of passion and zeal. She is artistic and academic. The world is a better place because she is here. I am grateful for this time with her at home before she launches out again. She is waiting on God for the next step in her journey. Though at times waiting is not easy, she knows that *"They that wait upon the Lord will renew their strength. They will mount up with wings like eagles; they will run and not get tired. They will walk and not become weary."* Isaiah 40:31 NASB

It is a beautiful autumn day here in Tennessee. The sun is shining. The leaves are changing colors. The air is cool. I am going to breathe in God's grace. I will see Him in the people I am with. I will hear Him in the wind in the trees. I will…*"taste and see that the Lord is good."* (Psalm 34:7).

It is a gift of life to me to be able to share some of the people and places that have been God's fragrance of grace to me.

This is an update since I first wrote this book. It is now March 2014. Bethany and Ben have three beautiful children. Elisha is 4 years old. Alethia is 2 years old and Alana is 4 months old. They are pure joy from God's heart to us! They are full of life and energy and joy! I am in love...

Celeste married Brandon Triola in September 2011. He is a gift to her and our family! He is fun loving, hard working and full of the love of Jesus. They are going to have a little Italian baby in November for me to love and spoil!

Charity has been living in Los Angeles since 2008. She has lived her dream to dance professionally. She has toured around the world and met wonderful people. She is full of life and laughter and creativity! Jesus shines through her heart! I am so proud to be her Mom.

Lately, I've been thinking about how God has brought me through it all, been with me in it all and has a purpose for it all. Lately, I've been thinking about God's love and faithfulness.

> *"For You have been my confidence from my youth. By You I have been sustained from my birth. You took me from my mother's womb."*
> (Psalm 71:5,6)

We have prayed this scripture as a family for years. I want to pray this over you too:

"The Lord bless you and keep you.
The Lord make His face shine upon you
and be gracious to you.
The Lord lift up His countenance upon
you and give you peace."
(Numbers 6:24-26)

If you have been blessed by this book, Rita would love to hear from you. You can email her at **ritabaroni77@gmail.com**

For information on Rita Baroni's ministry, to schedule her for speaking and ministry engagements, or to order her teaching downloads and music CDs, go to www.davidbaroni.com

To order additional copies of **"Fragrance of Grace"** *please email us at david@davidbaroni.com or order online at www.davidbaroni.com*

Made in the USA
Columbia, SC
23 February 2020